YOU *Are* POWERFUL!

ELLISHA T. NEWTON, M. Ed.

Book design by Ellisha T. Newton, M. Ed.

ISBN: 979-8-9885334-3-6 (Paperback)
ISBN: 979-8-9885334-2-9 (Hardcover)
ISBN: 979-8-9885334-1-2 (eBook)

Printed in the United States of America.

First paperback edition June 2023

Renewed Spirit Publishing
2245 Texas Drive
Suite 300
Sugar Land, Texas 77479-1679
www.RenewedSpiritPublishing.org

For more information contact:
Ellisha T. Newton, M. Ed.
info@RenewedSpiritPublishing.org

DEDICATION

This book is dedicated to my family and all the people in my village who contributed to me being the person I am today. Without you, I would not be possible.

Ellisha Tannee'

TABLE OF CONTENTS

PREFACE

"You Are Powerful!" is a book designed for readers aged 3 and above, emphasizing the inherent strength present in both young minds and seasoned scholars.

Vibrant and engaging illustrations adorn its pages, complemented by a glossary that enriches the reading experience. Apart from its empowering text, this book ensures that readers of all ages can enjoy, share, and explore art and a special surprise. (hint: music!)

As the author, I penned "You Are Powerful!" with the aim of inspiring readers to recognize and harness their inner strength. This book encourages individuals to not only embrace their personal power, but also to share it with others, engage in self-reflection, partake in educational endeavors, and formulate actionable plans.

Ultimately, the goal is to empower readers to make a positive impact on the world through their actions.

Ellisha T. Newton
Author, "You Are Powerful!"

"Write the vision and make it plain!"

~Habakkuk 2:2~

This illustration was created to depict the likenesses of the author as a little girl and her brother, Derek Woods, being encouraged by ancestors, that they are powerful. The author reminds readers they are powerful as well.

1

You are
POWERFUL!

The author's paternal grandfather, Ellis Woods, Sr. said, "The thing I loved to do as a child is play!" He always encouraged others to live life well. They watched how he worked and provided for his family. Through his actions he taught them they were loved!

3

You are
LOVED.

GOD LOVES YOU!

This cartoon is of a photo of the author as a little girl with her afro! When her Daddy styled her hair this was his favorite hairstyle to style for her!

You are
YOU!

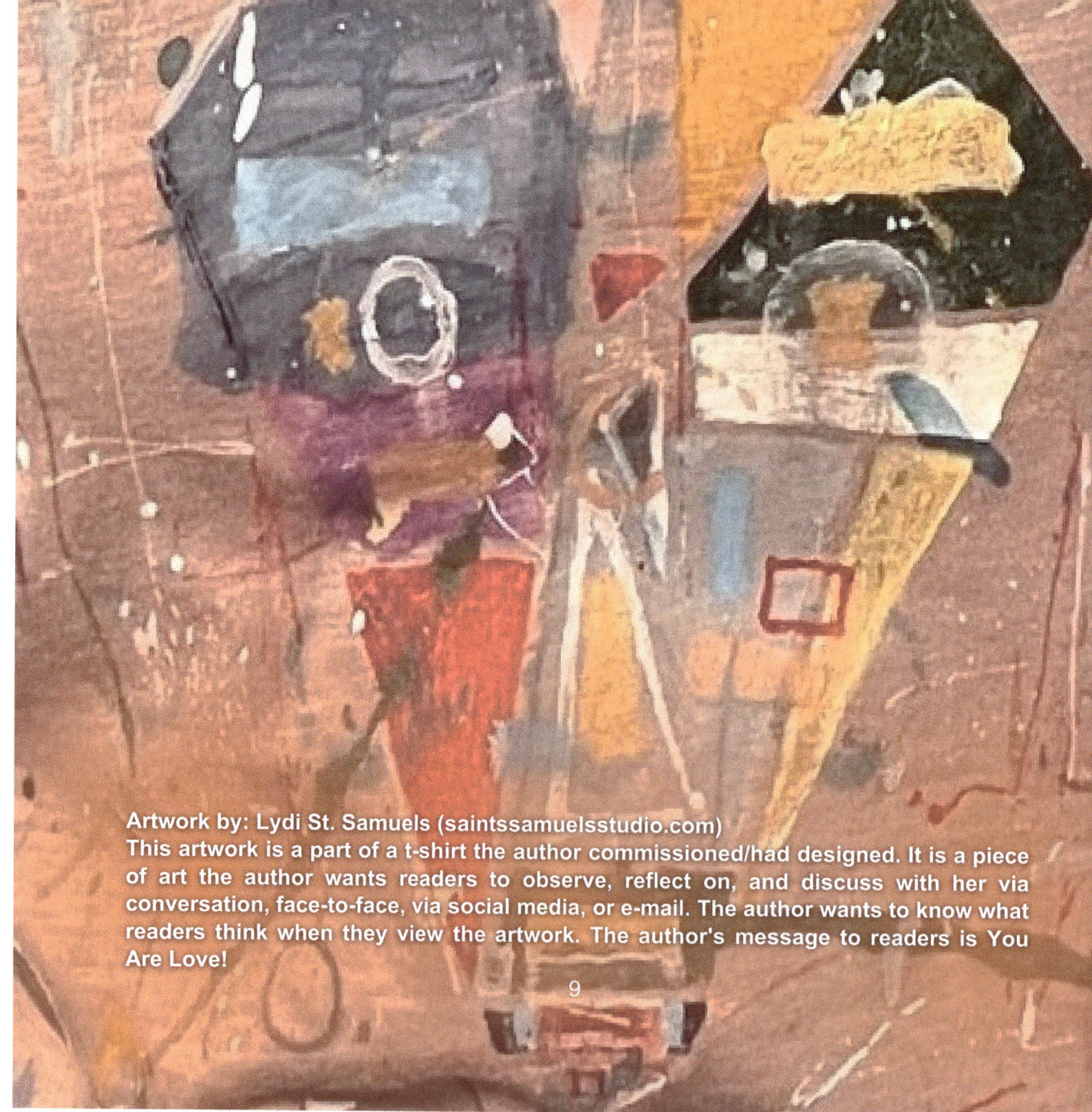

Artwork by: Lydi St. Samuels (saintssamuelsstudio.com)
This artwork is a part of a t-shirt the author commissioned/had designed. It is a piece of art the author wants readers to observe, reflect on, and discuss with her via conversation, face-to-face, via social media, or e-mail. The author wants to know what readers think when they view the artwork. The author's message to readers is You Are Love!

You are
LOVE.

This cartoon was created from the author's son, Sean Newton, Jr.' s young boy photo to depict to readers that their power can be seen in them by being themselves authentically.

I see your

POWER.

This cartoon was created of the author's husband, Mr. Sean Newton, Sr.' s youth photo to describe to readers that their greatness can been seen in them as a young person or as an adult.

13

I see the
GREATNESS
in you.

This cartoon was created from the author's son, Ethan Newton's young boy photo, to remind readers that God created them just as they are. This knowledge should encourage and assure them that they are not just good enough. In God's eyes, they are great!

God created
YOU
just like you
ARE.
That is not just
good enough,
that is
GREAT!

This illustration was created to depict the likeness of the author as a little girl being encouraged by ancestors that she is GREAT. The author reminds readers they are GREAT.

17

God

Reveres

Everything

About you AND your

Talents

19

Do you

SEE

the

GREATNESS

I see in you?

This illustration that depicts the author's maternal grandfather, Elijah Tann's likeness is included to encourage readers to "let the world see your greatness". Elijah Tann is the author's mother, Beatrice Woods' father.

21

Let the
WORLD
see your
GREATNESS.

SHINE

for all the world
to see!

The author's paternal uncle Samuel Woods is always positive, encourages everyone to express their feelings, asks how they are doing, and is geniunely concerned for all people. His image is included to encourage readers to let their light shine. (The author reminds readers that God's love is the light others see in us.)

25

Let your
LIGHT
shine.

This illustration was created to depict Mr. and Mrs. W.C. and Beatrice Taylor, the author's maternal grandparents' likenesses, because they impacted the author greatly. During her entire life's journey growing up as a little girl, as a young adult, and as an adult she learned from their examples that she should "stand tall". W.C. Taylor is the author's mother, Beatrice Woods's step father. Beatrice Taylor is the author's grandmother, Beatrice Woods' mother.

27

STAND
TALL!

Mrs. Ida Williams, the author's maternal great grandmother, Beatrice Taylor's mother.

Mr. Enoch Williams, the author's maternal great grandfather, Beatrice Taylor's father.

Woods Family (author's paternal grandparents, aunts, and uncles) - Back Row: Ellis Woods, Jr., (author's father), Uncles Robert and Ronald, and Aunt Mary Woods Copeland; Front Row, Ellis Woods Sr. and Mrs. Simmie Woods (grandparents), and Aunt Harriet.

The photos depicted here are created from the author's family photos; they capture the author's maternal and paternal great-grandparents, grandparents, parents, as well as uncles and aunts.

These ancestors inspired the author to understand her own power and greatness, and encouraged her to stand with her head up high.

The author encourages the readers to stand with their heads up high as well.

Mr. and Mrs. Ellis and Simmie Lee Woods, the author's paternal grandparents.

Mrs. Beatrice Taylor holding Beatrice Woods as a baby, the author's maternal grandmother and mother.

29

Stand with your head up HIGH.

This illustration was created from a photo of Morris Brown, the author's paternal great - grandfather. The words "Stand with your shoulders back" are encouragement for readers. Morris Brown is the father of Ellis Woods, Sr., the author's paternal grandfather. Ellis Woods, Sr. is the father of the author's father, Ellis Woods, Jr.

31

STAND

with your
shoulders back.

This illustration is of the author's maternal great - grandfather, John Tann, who exemplified with his life what it means to "Operate in excellence".

33

Operate in
EXCELLENCE.

This photo was taken by the author at the top of mountains in Estes Park, Colorado. It provides insight to readers that whether they are at the "top of a mountain" (at their highest points in life) or at their lowest points, whatever they go through, God is with them.

God is with you at

ALL TIMES.

You are God's best creation!

You are God's
BEST!

THE END

APPENDIX A

Glossary

You're Amazing (song written by the author)

Learning Activities - Definition of Terms

Learning Activities - Instructions

Journal Prompts

GLOSSARY

Definitions are in alphabetical order and are in relation to their meaning conveyed by the author.

01. **_Efficacious_** - is having a _special quality_ or _virtue_ and being _capable_ of _achieving_ anything you set your mind to do.

02. **Excellence** - is the powerful way you stand tall, tell the truth, hold your head up, look others in the eyes when you speak, and speak loudly and proudly.

03. **Greatness** - means you will be great and do great things in the world.

04. **Integrity** - is when you tell the truth and do what is right.

05. **Loved** - means there are people who love you.

06. **Love** - is the feeling of your heartbeat.

07. **Operate** - relates to the way you do everything.

08. **Quality** - is the best of the best.

09. **Powerful** - means mighty and efficacious.

10. **Power** -   is possessing strength.

11. **Shine** -   relates to your inner light that others see. That light is God's love shining through you.

12. **Special** - means you are unique.

13. **Truth** -   is the action of saying the words to tell what really happened.

14. **Unique** - means there is no one else like you. Simply put, unique means you are amazing!

15. **Virtue** - relates to being full of integrity and truth.

Now that you have read the glossary, proceed to page 43, follow the directions, and sing the song, **"You're Amazing!"**

You're Amazing! Instructions - Part 1

Sing the song **"You're Amazing!"**, then follow the Part 2 Directions located below the sheet music.

You're Amazing!

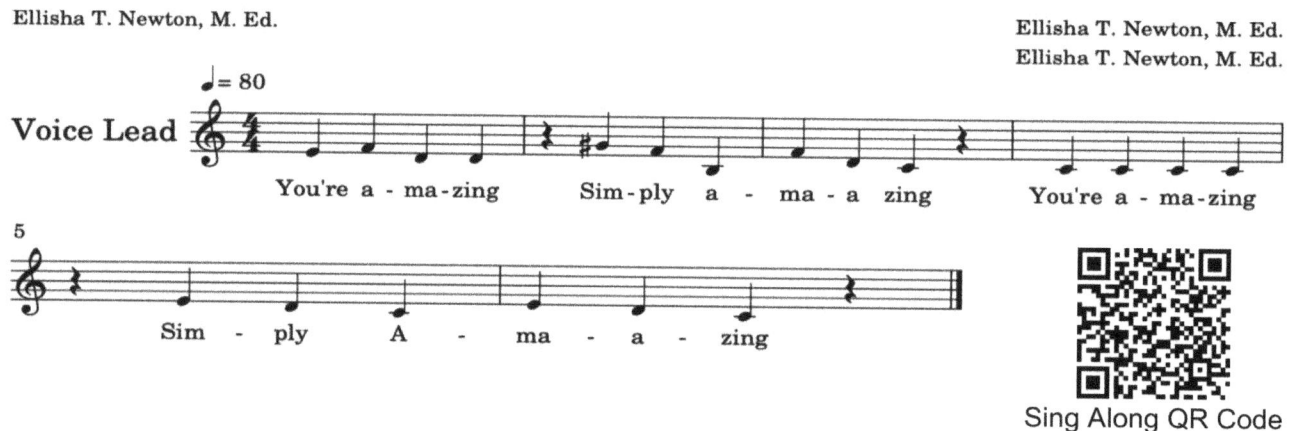

Sing Along QR Code

You're Amazing! Instructions- Part 2

Now that you have sung the song, **"You're Amazing!"** begin to reflect on what amazing means to you. In the space provided in the Journal Prompts, write and/or draw what amazing means to you.

43

Learning Activities
Definition of Terms

01. **Cadence** - a pattern using a melody or rhythm to close a musical phrase or song.

02. **Characteristics** - a way to describe something or someone.

03. **Close** - to bring parts together.

04. **Collaborate** - to work together to complete a task.

05. **Combination** - to join something together.

06. **Describe** - to explain something using words.

07. **Evidence** - the way you use words, photos, pictures, videos, or interviews to show your solution to the problem you are helping someone to solve or fix.

08. **Individual -** intended for one person.

09. **Join** - to bring something close together.

10. **Melody** - the leading part of a song with harmony.

11. **Musical score** - written music showing the individual parts.

12. **Part** - a specific voice or instrument in music.

13. **Problem** - something that has gone wrong.

14. **Qualities** - characteristics.

15. **Rap** - a poem set to music using a specific cadence.

16. **Research** - use evidence to show your solution to the problem you are helping someone to solve or fix.

17. **Resources** - things, people, or sources, you use and/or choose to collaborate to complete a task.

18. **Same** - something identical or similar to another.

19. **Similar** - having qualities in common.

20. **Set** - to add to something. (Example: Rap is a poem set to or added to music.)

21. **Solution** - the answer to a problem.

22. **Sources** - places, materials, resources, or people you use and/or with whom you choose to collaborate to complete a task.

23. **Specific** - a clear example.

24. **Tools** - things, ways of thinking, or thoughts you use to complete a task.

25. **Use** - the way to help someone to complete a task.

26. **Utilize** - a synonym that means to use.

27. **Wrong** - not correct or right.

Learning Activities

Instructions: Choose one or more of the activities below.

♡ Create an addition to the song "You're Amazing!"

♡ Create an addition to the song "You're Amazing!" that honors someone you know. Do you want to use your person's name in the song?

♡ Add a musical score to the song, "You're Amazing!"

♡ Think about the decision you made to create a song, play, book, rap, etc. What will you do next to add action to your plan?

♡ When teaching someone else what you created, what does the person or people need to do, consider, plan, implement, read, write, or research to add action to your plan?

♡ What tools do you suggest the person or people need to add action to your plan?

♡ What do you suggest that those people should consider eating or drinking, and where will they add action to your plan?

♡ What are some reasons you make the suggestions you have made to the people who are adding action to your plan?

Journal Prompts

USE A JOURNAL OR SOME OTHER PAPER TO WRITE THE ANSWERS TO THE FOLLOWING QUESTIONS.

Write and/or draw descriptions of how you are powerful.

Write and/or draw descriptions about how you are loved.

Write and/or draw descriptions about how God loves you.

Write and/or draw descriptions about how being you, looks, sounds, and feels.

Write or draw descriptions of how you know God is with you at all times.

Write and/or draw descriptions about being loved.

Write and/or draw descriptions about what you think when you view the artwork on page 9.

Write and/or draw descriptions about the power in you.

Write and/or draw descriptions about the greatness in you.

Write and/or draw descriptions about how you shine.

Write and/or draw descriptions of what amazing means to you.

Write and/or draw descriptions of how you know you are God's best.

APPENDIX B

Acknowledgments

Special Dedication

Additional Credits

About the Author

Order Copies

Contact Us

ACKNOWLEDGMENTS

I acknowledge my family and all the people in my village who contributed to me being the person I am today.

I thank my husband Sean, and our sons, Sean and Ethan. Your love and support are invaluable. I love you!

I thank my parents, Ellis Woods, Jr. and Annie Beatrice Woods, your love is unmatched. Thank you for being your genuine selves and surrounding me with a wonderful village growing up. I thank my mother - in - law, Brenda Belvin, and aunt Bridjette Perry for loving me, y'all mean the world to me. I thank my brother Derek Woods and sister-in-love, Shannon Woods. I love you! I can always count on you for fun and lots of laughter!

I thank my uncles, Robert Woods, Felton McCant, and Ronald Tann, my cousin, Johnsie Stewart, my aunts, LaVerne McCant, Mary Ellis Pitts, and Mary Copeland, for your contributions through family stories, photographs, research, and updated lineage.

I acknowledge my godfather, Julius Mines, my godsister, Arlene Brown, godbrothers, James Brown, Basil Smith, Clyde Dyson, and my aunts Harriett Woods, Kathy Woods, Helen White, Rabiyah Crichton, my uncle Samuel Woods, my cousins, nieces, nephews, friends, and my entire village, thank you for being authentically you. I am because you are.

I salute my great-grandparents, grandparents, great-uncles, Lafayette Williams, P.R. Gaines, Fred Gaul, Robert Woods: great aunts, Mamie Hood, Lillie Bell Porter, Shellie Gaines, Frednell Coleman; my uncle Ronald Woods, godmother, Cleo Mines, and my godsisters, Thea Smith and Theda Dyson.

I appreciate all of the ancestors who have gone to be with the Lord.

Elisha T. Newton

Author, "You Are Powerful!"

SPECIAL DEDICATION

This book is further dedicated to:

~Great-Grandparents~
Mr. and Mrs. Enoch and Ida Beatrice Stafford Williams,
Mr. and Mrs. John and Annie Nesmith Tann,
and Mr. and Mrs. Morris and Mary Brown,

~Grandparents~
Mr. and Mrs. Ellis and Simmie Lee Stewart Woods, Sr.
and
Mr. Elijah Tann,
Mr. and Mrs. W.C. and Beatrice Williams Taylor,
and all the ancestors.

Without you, I would not be possible.

ADDITIONAL CREDITS

The illustrations were created from photos that were utilized with permission from each person in the photos and/or the executors of the person's estates.

The cartoons were created using Toon App.

Photo Credit
The cartoon on page 35 was created from an original photo taken by Eureka Woods.

The photo on page 60 was taken by Ethan Newton.

The photo on page 64 was taken by Taylor M. Hayden of TMH Creative, taylormhayden.com.

The illustrations for **You Are Powerful!** were created by Christian Rodriguez and the team at YourChildren'sBook.com.

ABOUT THE AUTHOR

Ellisha Newton, M. Ed., is an author, global speaker, and consultant who specializes in leading and building teams. Mrs. Newton crafts environments where all adult and youth leaders assist scholars in thriving through Literacy in Science, Technology, Engineering, and Mathematics. (S.T.E.M.) Consequently, scholars demonstrate their literacy as they teach others what they are learning.

Mrs. Newton models high levels of competent, caring, and culturally responsive collaboration. In her 28+-year tenure in the field of education, she has led as an Educator in Pre-K - 8th Grade and in administration at campus, school district, and higher education levels.

In her book, "How to Love Your Job Daily for Educators: 7 Secrets to Understanding Health = Wealth", Ellisha Newton, M. Ed. assists leaders in reaching their goals while mentoring others. In her upcoming book, "Light!" Mrs. Newton encourages readers to use the science concepts, life lessons, and journal prompts to document and reflect on their multi-disciplinary connections to light.

ORDER COPIES

To order more copies of
"You Are Powerful!"
go to RenewedSpiritPublishing.org and click Shop.

Utilize the QR Code below to order the book, "You Are Powerful!" as well.

FREE GIFT

Thank you for purchasing,
You Are Powerful!

Redeem your free gift, a 15 Minute Discovery call!
To schedule a Discovery Call at your convenience today, go to
RenewedSpiritPublishing.org and click Discovery Call.

Utilize the QR Code below to schedule your Discovery Call as well.

YOU *Are* POWERFUL!

ELLISHA T. NEWTON, M. Ed.

www.RenewedSpiritPublishing.org

Want to invite the author to speak at your school district, school, conference, workshop, event, or to your group?
Go to the website or email:

info@RenewedSpiritPublishing.org

Renewed Spirit Publishing
2245 Texas Drive
Suite 300
Sugar Land, Texas 77479-1679

ISBN: 979-8-9885334-2-9 (Hardcover) | ISBN: 979-8-9885334-3-6 (Paperback)

www.ingramcontent.com/pod-product-compliance
Lightning Source LLC
Chambersburg PA
CBHW041124120626
46547CB00019B/2841